presentation of the information is without contract or any type of guarantee assurance.

The trademarks that are used are without any consent, and the publication of the trademark is without permission or backing by the trademark owner. All trademarks and brands within this book are for clarifying purposes only and are the owned by the owners themselves, not affiliated with this document.

TABLE OF CONTENTS

Introduction

The mind is the powerhouse of human being that enables consciousness, thinking, perception, judgment, and memory. On the other hand, Character is the mental and moral qualities distinctive to every being.

When the two are combined, they define the personality in someone. However, the life we are living today is defined by the thoughts in one's mind and the action implemented on the outside to be who we are.

There is a lot of information that has been shared on the subject, but this guide is more of suggestive than an explanation. The aim of this book is to stimulate readers to discover the potential in their thoughts and apply the shared information in their daily lives.

Thanks for buying this Book, I hope you enjoy it!

Chapter 1

Impact of Thought on General Well Being

The body is a delicate and plastic instrument, it is a follower of the mind, and thus it does what the mind directs it to do. Whether the command is deliberate or expressed automatically, it has to adhere to the instructions. When the body is under a control of good thoughts, it becomes garbled with beauty and youthfulness. In layman's language, we can say, people who have good emotional health and are acutely aware of their thoughts, behavior, and feeling, are the ones who have learned ways on how to cope with stress, anxiety and daily problems which are part and parcel of life.

However, if you summon your body with unlawful thoughts, the body will deteriorate and be engulfed with diseases, worry and it will sink into them rapidly. Negative thoughts are rooted and originate from the mind, and they are conveyed clearly when the body is sick. Negative thoughts have been known to cause more harm to the body, and in fact, they kill a man at a rocket speed, and they are still killing thousands of people. Individuals who are prone to suffer from negative thoughts are those who live in fear.

Anxiety plays a major part in demoralizing the body as it leaves the body and mind wide open to the access of diseases. If you continue to propagate foul thoughts, your body will continue to have immoral and poisoned blood. A clean mind and heart will give birth to a clean body. Every action is palpable of thought because; thought is the source of action and life.

Even if you switch to a healthy diet, without changing your thoughts, it is equal to dressing a white hen socks. But once your thoughts are pure, the change of diet will be just an additional ingredient. Good habits emanate from good thoughts. On the flip side, the vice versa is the replica. Therefore, guarding the mind is as important as perfecting your body. It is unfortunate that the majority are overwhelmed with envy, disappointment, malicious and despondency thoughts which burglarize the health and grace of the body.

It is possible to improve on emotions only if you understand your feelings and how you control them. Also, you need to know the cause of your anxiety, sadness and stress. This way, you will be able to maintain your emotional health. Living a balanced life is one way you can control your emotions. Today's life is moving at a bullet speed and because of many activities like schoolwork, problems at work can all lead to negative feelings. Instead of pretending to be happy and yet you are stressed, upset or anxious. Although it is advisable to deal with these negative feelings, focusing on positive things in your life is what you need to do. You also have to let go of some things in your life, those that make you feel overwhelmed and stressed.

Calm your mind and body using methods like meditation to bring emotions back to balance. Also, we earlier saw that people who live in fear are the ones who are affected mostly by negative thoughts, thus developing resilience is imperative. People who are resilient have better a chance of coping with stress in a healthy way. Then again, know how you can express your feelings because good changes can be as stressing as bad habits.

Chapter 2

How Thought and Character Are Related

The epigram of mind does not only clutch and define who a man is but it encompasses all elements because it reaches out to every circumstance of his life. The character of a man is the summation of what he thinks. In essence, he is what he thinks.

Just like a plant can emanate from nowhere without sowing seeds the mentality of every man stems from hidden seeds of thoughts which could not have appeared without them. This applies equally to the unplanned and unrehearsed persons who are purposively accomplished.

The actions of someone are fruits of thought which are either suffering or joy. In essence, a man reaps the fruits of his thoughts, whether sweet or bitter. The man is not a duplicate of creation rather a growth by law. Therefore, belief and consequences are pure and readily available in the kingdom of thoughts just like in the world of visible and material things. The decency in a man is a natural result of positive thinking. A righteous and good quality is not a favor rather it's a natural consequence of one having a positive perception in every doing. On the other hand, a despicable and subhuman mentality, by the same process is as a result of continuous fostering of lying thoughts.

A man is nurtured by himself. Within his weaponry of thoughts, he simulates a weapon by which he destroys by himself. He also mode the tool through which, he constructs his Vatican of joy and strength and peace. By making the right decisions and applying them appropriately, man can climb to the delightful perfection. But if he applies his thoughts in a wrong way, he will descend below the level of recognition. These two antipodes are all the set of class of character, and man is the epicenter.

Of all the good deeds associated with the soul, some which have been brought to light at this age and some which have been restored, none is delighting and assertive than this- the man is the monarch of thought, the sculpture of character, the builder and caster of the environment, condition, and destiny.

A man holds the key to every state despite being of power, intelligence, and love and the mogul of his own thoughts. Within himself, he has metamorphosed, and an occurring agency by which he makes what he intends. Even during a fragile and abandoned situation, man is always the ruler. But on the flip side, during this time (weakness and degradation) he is also the one who inefficiently misguide his thoughts. When he reviews the condition and can be manifested by him starting from his soul.

There is a universal norm in being that a successful person oppresses the unsuccessful. This norm can be erased and reversed. The problem is that the unsuccessful individuals submit to the views and ideas of the successful hoping to be successful as they are. However, the fact that majority fail to understand is that the successful just like the unsuccessful both suffer in away and it is a result of them. This fact is not understood, and the bitter truth is that the ignorance of the wicked is as poisonous as the might of the successful. We all make mistakes against creational laws, and there is no reason to berate one another. Humanity must be raised between the two parties.

You can emerge victorious only if you can rise, defeat and have positive thinking. If you don't, you will subject yourself to weakness, lamentable and wretched lifestyle. Nothing comes on a bed of roses, and before you can achieve your goals, you must have a positive thinking excluding, anxiety, stress, pro-crastination and the likes. Two factors are to be put to the test, if not sacrificed in order to succeed. These are selfishness and antipathy. In any case, your mind is bound by barbaric gratification; no way will you think the right path neither will you have an effective plan.

You will not utilize underlying wealth, and you will be an epic failure in every undertaking.

For you to achieve your every undertaking, it narrows down to one thing: thought. You need to control your thoughts so that you can be able to control all your affairs at the same time to revamp sober responsibilities. Every life achievement you have to pay an ultimate price which is a sacrifice. Success in most cases is measured by the sacrifices one undertakes plus self-confidence and right decision making. The higher you set your ambitions, the commitment you remain in achieving them, the greater chances of achieving them.

Among us, there are those who are greedy, dishonest and inhuman and the world does not favor such personalities although, on the flip side, it may seem to favor them. The universe has and will always favor the saintly, honest and philanthropic beings. Great minds of all time have expressed this in different ways and as an individual, you can prove this through persistent decision making and lifting your thoughts.

Psychological achievement is as a result of searching for knowledge. In some cases, these achievements are as a result of egotism and aspiration, but they are not related to one's character. These are natural fruits from a laborious effort free from selfless thoughts.

Holy aspirations will give birth to spiritual achievements. A person who has been raised and nurtured in a spiritual environment, and has the aspiration of becoming a saint, and at the time of maturation, the character will have grown in him/her and will rise to help the less blessed.

Any success originates from the soul and then supported by self-control, integrity, righteousness and positive thinking. Confusion, worry, impurity, corruption, indolence and barbaric thoughts are ingredients of failure. The thought factor in achievement is directed by the thought which emanates from your mind, led and governed by the same law. If your wish is to accomplish much, you need to sacrifice much and vice versa. You have to sacrifice greatly to attain highly.

Chapter 4

Agitation and Peace

We all feel satisfied, have an inner peace of mind and feel happy when life flows smoothly. All these will result in having good relationships, good health, and good job not to mention a stable financial situation. We have nothing to worry about, no tension, anxiety, stress and no hurry. For your mind to be calm, you need to exercise self-control and patience. When someone is calm and has a peace of mind, it is clear that person is mature and has vast experience more than ordinary knowledge governing the operation of thoughts.

You need to understand yourself to be calm. By doing so, you will be able to understand others as a result of thought and correct thinking. Although life change on a daily basis, there is always something that will cause tension, worry, and fear that will result in being not to have a peace of mind, never-theless, you can enjoy peace regardless of the outer circumstances.

A calm person is that person who was cultured to control himself and knows how to interact with different souls. Those around him will appreciate his spiritual strength. Such people are the ones you feel like you ought to rely on and learn from them. The more calm you become, the more successful you become, the more your influential and power you attain. A good example is have you realized the majority of people prefer buying from that vendor who has self-control of his business and is always calm? The reason is that people prefer dealing with someone whose attitude is relaxed.

People will always admire and respect you only if you are calm and stable. You will be like an oasis in the desert. To attain inner serenity and peace of mind, you will need to put together all that has been discussed from the first chapter. Let me sum them up here. We can all learn a new language, but the level of expertise of each will be different right? We can engage in various activities but at the end, the results will not be the same. But at least, each will reach a different level. All these depends on your inner soul, the sincerity of yourself and the time you devoted yourself to these activities. So, it is through training that you will be free from pressure and intimidation of unremitting thinking that you will attain peace of mind.

Many people have ruined their lives because of the explosive temper; they have destroyed that good character in them because of lack of self-control. How many people do we meet that have a balanced life? Those who have characters that everyone admire and would like to associate with them? If you feel agitated, try to calm your mind. Take one step back and look at your mind as if you were looking for someone. It is through self-control that you will strength. It is through calmness that you will attain power. All these actions will calm your mind and make it serene.

Chapter 5

Illusion and Perfection

In the earlier chapter, we saw that survivors of the world are those who cherish their dreams. The world is visible but funny enough it is sustained by the invisible. The invisible are the idea, thoughts that we beings generate in our souls to be better now and in future. The dreams and visions you have in your mind are invisible that govern the universe. It is hard for humanity to forget their ancestors. To prove this, even in today's life, we still use theories that were discovered by scientist 20-30 years back. Beings cannot let their dreams fade away. They live in them hoping one day their dreams will come into reality.

Makers of the world are poets, prophets, sculptors and many others who have lived in this world before. Without them, humanity would easily perish but because these makers had dreams and visions, and they are still in us and living by them.

If you adore alluring vision at your heart, one day it will come into reality. Admire your visions, ideal, your beauty in your heart and any good thing that you know has a positive impact on your life, because out of it, a delightful condition will emerge, but on the condition that you are yourself and remain true to them.

In real life, if you have for long desired to have something, you will have to work extremely hard to get that thing, so, do what you desire to obtain and you have to aspire to achieve. No shameful mind will receive satisfaction, and an unpolluted ambition will never lack nourishment. The law is very clear, ask and you will be given, search and you will find; work hard and you will succeed. No shortcut.

Always dream big because dreams are seeds of realities. At times, you might be in the unpleasant situation, but it won't last long if you can realize the unachievable and strive to achieve it. The tactless, lazy and unlettered when the visibly see the effects of one's vision and ideals, you hear them talking about how lucky one is and not them. When someone becomes rich, they talk about how lucky that person is and easily forget the struggles and failures he has gone through.

Such people have no idea how to sacrifice themselves, how to put efforts in something that they would like to achieve and how to exercise patience for them to conquer the unconquerable and realize their visions a heart. They have no clued that for you to succeed, you must be ready to tackle all the taunting hurdles you come across, but they only think that everything is by luck. They in most cases sit back and wait for everything to drop from heaven instead of walking the talk. Nothing comes on a silver plate, and that is a fact!

All these people, whom we see as successful, they have tirelessly worked for their success and those whom we see lazing around, are those who keep wishing and saying that the successful were lucky. It's high time you need to get out of your comfort zone, get the romance out of your mind and cherish your dreams because it is only glorifying the visions in your mind, and the idea that you install in your heart is the way you will build your life and become successful.

Chapter 6

Feeling and Justification

There is no intuitive accomplishment until the thought is linked with purpose. The majority of people are usually moved by life changes because they live by the day. Few have a purpose in life and those that don't have, are the once swept by these life changes.

According to philosopher James Allen in his book "As a Man Thinketh" he states that a man who has no paramount purpose in life is an ingredient to worries, fears, self-pitying, and troubles all which are signs of weakness. When all these are summed up, the results are unplanned actions which will lead to unhappiness, loss, failure and weakness which persist in the fast changing world.

We human beings we are supposed to devise a meaningful purpose in our hearts and embark on accomplishing it. The purpose conceived should be the streamline of our thoughts. Depending on the nature of being, the purpose might take the form of a spiritual idea or a worldly object. Once you embark on accomplishing your purpose, make it the main agenda and all your concentration should be focused on achieving the ultimate goal.

Consign yourself and don't allow your thoughts to be swayed away with imaginations, longings, and fleeting fancies. This should mark the cornerstone to self-control and true concentration of thoughts. The outcome is either victory or failure, but even if you fail several times on achieving the set purpose, you should not give up until you overcome your weakness. And, this will form a new starting point in your life for future accomplishments.

It is not easy to achieve a purpose in life, and if you are not prepared for consternation, you better prepare your thoughts for an impeccable performance no matter how trifling the purpose may appear. It is only through taking this route that you will be able to gather your thoughts, remain focused, for energy and resolution to be developed. Once you accomplish this, there is no hurdle that you can't jump. A weak mind will only believe in this theory that strength can be developed through effort and practice once it starts to deploy its strength and put them into practice. In essence, practice makes it perfect. It is at this point that when you have a keen intellect, you will realize effort, patience and strength will develop in your mind. Those who are physically weak can develop themselves to be strong by careful patient training, which means people with weak thoughts can be strong by exercising the right thinking.

To get rid of purposeless and fragility is the stepping stone to enter a class of the successful people who don't see failure as a hindrance rather as a motivating factor to achieving their set goals. When you fail, you learn something which you didn't know and from it, you stand up, dust yourself and tackle the issue with ferocious strength. However, you must be able to tackle the set purpose fearlessly, and think strongly to accomplish it successfully.

Achieving a purpose in life has proved a hard task to achieve to the majority, but a shrewd process has to be implemented. Don't look left, right or back but your mind should be focused on the laid path. Fears and doubts will be encountered, but you should exclude them from your mind. The two plus anxiety and lack of confidence will shatter your efforts in achieving your purpose. Once you allow your mind to be fooled by fears and doubts, you can hardly achieve anything apart from failure. They will suppress your purpose, efforts, power, and energy.

Doubts and fear are great enemies of knowledge, and this draws a line between achievement and failure. If you can vanquish fear and doubt, you have trounced failure. Your mind will have the ultimate power to overcome all difficulties you may encounter in life.

It needs one to have a purpose in life, have a positive thinking and lay a pathway on how you achieve your set purpose, excluding the mentioned factors to be successful. That is how thought and purpose are linked.

Chapter 7

Upshot of Thoughts on Daily Events

The mind of a man can be compared to the garden which can be refined or be left to run wild. But whether it is cultivated or not, it must yield the outcome. If functional seeds are not sowed into it, then prepare to reap useless weed-seeds, and the trend will continue after that.

Let us take into reality. A gardener will maintain his plot by cultivating it to keep it free from weeds and plants flowers and fruits which he expects a good harvest. So, does a man develop his mind as well weed off evil thoughts, useless and wicked thoughts, and instead plant useful flowers and fruits of right thoughts. It is only through chasing this process that a man will discover he is the chief-gardener of his soul and the manager of his life. In so doing, he will be able to disclose the flow of thoughts within himself, understand with the increasing accuracy, how the forces of thought and mind element operate in mentoring the character, fortune, and circumstances.

The character and thoughts are summed up as one thing. A character can only be evident and uncover itself through circumstances and environment. The outer doings or condition of a man in most cases is compatible with his inner state. This should not be a summation of a man circumstances at any given time that it is an indication of his entire character rather those situations are closely related with the vital thought element within himself and for the time being they are imperative to his development.

Every man is where he is because of the law of his being. He is where he is because of the thoughts he has built in his character. And when you narrow deep down to the arrangement of his life, there is no element of chance but due to a law which cannot be mistaken. To those who are contented with the environment in which they are, and those who feel out of amity, this is true.

As a man continues to grow, he progressively learns spiritual lessons in every situation he comes across which gives a place to another situation. A man is bothered by several situations but the only way to overcome them is by believing in him, having a positive thinking and cultivating the culture of optimism. This way he will be able to realize that he can overcome difficult situations and emerge the winner. It simply means that we can influence our circumstances by simply taking a stun action from the epicenter of the situation. When we remain bothered with situations, we feel pity of ourselves and feel less fortunate, feeling nostalgia on some occasions why all bad deed take part in our lives without a substantial reason. We ought to understand that we are the creators of these circumstances. Therefore, it is important to practice self-control and self-punctuation.

It should be noted that every thought planted in the mind and allowed to spread will have an effect on the outcome character sooner or later. If you get obsessed with evil thoughts, expect the outcome to be negative and if you plant good thoughts, expect good fruits. A man starts to realize he is a man when he stops to whimper and castigate. And instead, search for the hidden justice within his soul which will regulate and streamline his life. Once he adapts the regulating factor in his mind, he halts blaming others for being the reason for his condition and builds himself a strong, reputable thought. Instead of abandoning the circumstance, he uses them to aid his progress to discover more powers.

By any chance you realize you have created a negative thought and moved on it, it is imperative that you look for that mental weakness that gave birth to it. The environment, on the other hand, will be the surgery room for a change of self where you have to allow these negative thoughts to be tackled in such a way that its reoccurrence will be blocked. This brings to what fighting against circumstance means? It means a man is in constant disgust against, anxious to improve on circumstance and not ready to improve on them. If we look at this behavior within ourselves, you will find that it is an uphill task to clinch victory without addressing negative thoughts within our mind and soul that can hinder the success. It is imperative that we focus, tame and exclude those things that prevent us from achieving success. It is where the idea of achieving results in every situation comes from only if we set our thoughts and confidently believe in them within our minds. Once we wholly understand this future success, reality itself will begin to change – a process known as selective shift.

This is when you will see the opportunities that went unnoticed now become visible. And people who seem to abandon us will start to gather resources to aid us to achieve our goals. Our thoughts change constantly, and each has an effect on our daily lives. The best thing to do is to understand these thoughts and align each with a similar set of goals. Fostering bad thoughts will not only prevent progress, but they will disorganize circumstances and work against us. We need to set goals and encrypt them in our minds, that way we will find the progress of each leading to the other.

At any given time if you present a negative thought, beware that it is your inability to handle it internally. Each time you eliminate a negative thought from your mind, the result that is associated with that thought will never occur in your life. This simply means when you progress into a strong thinker, you do away with negative thoughts which might enter your life, thus, you can face any new challenge and take it as an opportunity to turn things around.

Chapter 8

Summary

We have different personalities, but the most important thing is to understand oneself. It is easier to ruin your personality with explosive anger, lack of patience and self-control.

Just like friendship or relationship takes time to nurture, you are the only one who can cultivate your character starting by having a positive motive from your mind.

Whatever emanates from your heart is the outcome of what you do.

Conclusion

Now that you've been presented with the basic ideas about how our thoughts shape us, it's time for you to put the remaining portion into practice. This is not a onetime practice but it is something you have to train yourself.

It is not late for you to achieve your goals in life when you change your perception and start thinking right as early as today!

Finally, if you enjoyed this book, then I'd like to ask you for a favor, would you be kind enough to leave a review for this book on Amazon? It'd be greatly appreciated!

Made in the USA
Lexington, KY
24 June 2016